DON'T CRY FOR ME

I'm Free... Atop a Piñon Tree

A Tribute to Rita Gilbert
By
Joyce Marie Gilbert

Published by Keystone Vortex Publishing, Rio Rancho, New Mexico

Gilbert, Joyce Marie
    Don't Cry For Me ... I'm Atop a Piñon Tree / Joyce Marie Gilbert

ISBN 978-0-9889662-2-2

PRINTED IN THE UNITED STATES OF AMERICA

First Edition

Dedication

In Memoriam, I'd like to dedicate this book to our sweet mother, Rita Aurora Gilbert who journeyed home on June 6, 2015.

Her life long commitment to God and her dedication to daily prayer is my inspiration for seeking God through a daily meditative writing practice.

In honor of our mother's deep passion for peace and unity for her family, I wish to dedicate this collection of Meditative Writings to her family....her most treasured possession.

It is with much appreciation and gratitude to my mother for guiding me through this pilgrim's journey into my soul.

Table of Contents

A BLESSED BLOW...72
A CELIBATE SPIRIT..15
A DAY OF BURIAL...97
A DAY OF GRATITUDE...7
A GOOD FRIDAY..98
A PERSONAL TRAIT...70
A STREET CAR NAMED DESIRE...............................17
ALLOW THYSELF TO BE TIRED...............................65
APART FROM ME..41
APPOINTMENT TO DINE...1
ASCEND...76
ASK FOR ME..77
BE THY SPACE..26
BEFORE THEE I STAND...39
BLESS THE CHILDREN..68
BLESS THE MOMENT..46
BLESS THE PEOPLE, OH LORD!................................19
CALM THY MIND...64
CAST OUT FEAR...29
CORPUS CHRISTY...95
DANCE OH MORNING!...75
DEEP IS CALLING ON DEEP.....................................20
DEEP SEEDS...37
DEPARTURE OF JUDGEMENT....................................50
DO NOT BE ANGUISHED...63
DO NOT TOUCH ME...60
EXTEND TO THOSE..55
FEAR NOT..6
GLORY IN THE WORLD..80
GOD-MADE CONNECTIONS.......................................3
HERE I AM, THY WILL BE DONE...............................25
HOW LOVELY IS YOUR DWELLING PLACE......................11

I TRULY KNOW..43
I WALK WITH THEE..59
IN THE STILLNESS..81
INTEGRES GRACE...51
LIFE IN THE DAY OF THE ROCK....................33
LISTEN OH GOD..94
LOST IN THE ONE WHO PROVOKES MY AWE..............96
MARY OH MOTHER..35
MORE OF THE SAME.....................................47
MY MOTHER...99
OF THIS I KNOW...62
OH FATHER!...69
OH FAULT!...52
OH HAPPY DAY...45
OH LOSS..38
OH PARACLETE...84
OIL OF GLADNESS...78
OMMISSIONS AND COMMISSIONS....................86
ON THIS DAY..90
ONLY HONOR..16
PASS..66
PASS ON..73
PERCOLATION OF VIRTUE...............................36
PONDER THE CROSS.....................................12
PONDER THE WONDER...................................34
PRAY OH GOD...85
PRAY OH GOD!..79
PRAYER WITHOUT A PRAYER..........................53
RAISE A GLAD CRY.......................................93
REDUCE MY SPACE...9
REPAIRER OF THE BREACH............................48
RETURN OH MOTHER...................................100
SACRED SPACE...22
SALUTE TO DARKNESS...................................88
SECRET RESURRECTIONS................................91
SELF REVENGE...82

ST. AGNUS..2
ST. CATHERINE..67
STILL ME...58
STILL TODAY..13
SUNSHINE ON MY FACE.. 14
TAMPERING WITH EVIDENCE...................................30
THE BATTLE OF THE ANGELS..................................49
THE BREATH IN THE STORM....................................61
THE DAY AFTER...101
THE DESIRE TO BE GOD..4
THE ENCOUNTER..31
THE GARDEN OF DELIGHT......................................42
THE GRACE OF NAKEDNESS....................................74
THE INTERFACE..71
THE JOY IN YOUR NAME..89
THE LOVE OF EMPTYNESS.......................................92
THE MOTION OF ENERGY..23
THE NAKED EYE...57
THE PONDER...5
THE PONDER OF THE DAY..44
THE QUIET MIND..54
THE SABBATH WITHIN..18
THE SHINING CLOUD...56
THE SPIRIT OF NUN...10
THE SPIRIT OF POVERTY...21
THE TOUCH OF THE HEART.....................................32
THE WOMAN WHO SPEAKS.....................................40
THIS ECLIPSE..87
THIS SUFFERING..83
TRANSCENDING MOVEMENT...................................27
WATER BLOOD AND SPIRIT......................................8
WHAT SACRIFICE IS THIS..24
WINTER IN PONDER..28

APPOINTMENT TO DINE

Happy oh God! I am, for the appointment to dine.
I look around all I see is the encampment of humanity
All who camp near your house
Fasten their tent pegs next to her walls.

Mother-like she welcomes us
Like a traveler long past....a security net to be cast

Encamped we are
Meditating on wisdom
Day and night
Pondering, pondering, pondering.

Joy and gladness we find
An everlasting home in our mind
Vanished tents of human kind
Happy I am oh God, for the appointment to dine
May my every moment be hosted by the Divine.

ST. AGNUS

Oh Chaste! Thy meekness has revealed your goodness
Thy eyes have seen its golden light
Remember the passion, recall the fight
Naked, imprisoned, raped and martyred
You are for us, life deferred
You are for us
Why it occurred.

Stand in the shadow of our death
Witness for us what we cannot acclaim
See our fall; for we are lame
Regard us not as one of your same
Intercede for us and raise our consciousness; for
We are the people, the banished children of Eve
Who through your goodness can conceive

May we rest in your state
Will you accept your fate
Accept this request; for it is pure
We ask you in earnest
For this cure.

GOD-MADE CONNECTIONS

Connect me oh God to your connections
Anoint the interface created by you
Direct my mind to mantras, minimize contras, and
Dissolve that which is not You.

Connect me oh God to the nothingness of your creation
Introduce me to all the peoples of this nation
I have traveled to my destination for this preparation
A birth be known, a child was shown, a trumpet blown
A connection to Creation
Burst through the moan.

A gift of heavenly worth
A chance to shed my curse
What child is this
Who birthed life into bliss.

An interface created, God and man was mated
Awaken Oh God!
For I have been illuminated.

THE DESIRE TO BE GOD

Star oh star wherever you are
The idea of my desire is not so far
Full of enlightenment so bright and so near
The fulfillment of perfection
Ever so clear.

Chancing the dance to dare to survive
Is my desire to be God; and I have arrived
To seek less, is God deprived
Stuck in a consciousness
Is self contrived.

Oh God, oh God you find me here
Awakened I am
The I am that I am
Existing in wholeness invested in truth
I am who you find
A seer
The God in the mirror.

THE PONDER

Accept me as the bride of ponder
May I never become apart
Of what God has put asunder
May I renounce my home down under...and
Roam in the realms of heavenly wonder.

The ponder, the ponder Oh! Holy Grail
Come with me through my days of frail
Lead me light years away from where I sail
Remind me not of my mind so blind
Nor of my days of human kind.

...but marry me now for I am yours
Carry me away in search of the search
Accept my journey as I build my church
Ponder the ponder for I am she
Recall the consciousness of the heavenly.

FEAR NOT

Take courage! Be the I am
I am the voice and the listener
I am the patient and practitioner
I am the seeker and the sought
Take courage
And fear not.

In this consciousness take my place
In the mirror I see no face
Only the I am that I am
Only the courage to be love
Only God, eternally
From above.

Fear not, for I am here
Replace thy sight with an eternal ear
Listen in courage not in fear
I am the I am
Your conscience....and
Your peer.

A DAY OF GRATITUDE

A day of light
A day of glow
Today is the day gratitude flows
A day to cheer up from all highs and lows.

Cheer up, cheer up the day has come
A time for cookies and hot buttered rum
A place of grace in this perfect place
Arise oh people!
We are no longer deaf and dumb.

A day to journey a day of fame
A dance and a prance
We're no longer lame
From the birth of the mother
and the death of the same
We my brother and sister
Are here to proclaim
We are journey we are spirit
Bless our mother
From where we came.

WATER BLOOD AND SPIRIT

What child is this?
Witnessed by water blood and spirit
Witnessed by those who dare it
In the kingdom I sit
In the presence I know
The spirit testifies
Here is where water and blood flow.

The Son of Man appears
The veil so sheer
I see myself in the mirror
Witness oh Spirit!
Awakened to those who dare it.

Arrived from journey
Here in the kingdom
Witnessed by water blood and spirit
Together we are those....
Who merit.

Joyce Marie Gilbert

REDUCE MY SPACE

I am the I am only to find me gone
I awakened today to the hum of this song
Alleluia to the idea that nothing could be wrong
Why did I entertain fear and doubt
For so long.

Reduce my space dismiss my case
Pluck me from the human race
Say the word
And I'll be awakened in
Another place
The I am that I am
Has pleaded my case.

My space reduced
God pursued
Only One is what I find here
Only God-space.....what's to fear
I am gone thou art near
Only God-space
In this mirror.

THE SPIRIT OF NUN

Some say Elijah some say John
No matter! is the spirit of Nun!
No matter whose mouth it's from
The spirit of nun
Is thy kingdom come.

Thy kingdom come has arrived for some
The beat of the drum is the OM
The sound of the OM is my home
OM is the home
Where the buffalo roam.

On earth as it is in heaven
The completion is the number 7
Receive from me the spirit of nun
Thy kingdom has arrived
You are now self-deprived
We, the I am exist in glory
The spirit of nun
Is where we're from.

HOW LOVELY IS YOUR DWELLING PLACE

Happy whose strength is in you
Whose hearts are on the road to Zion
The bitter valley we can rely on
....but the Son of Man whose
Shoulders we cry on.

A place of spring
Oh winter shed your blessing
I feel your caressing
Wrap your cold press
Against my heart
Oh bitter valley swallow me up
Do thy part.

But happy I am
Whose heart is on the road to Zion
But strong am I at the trial and tribulation
My heart sings with the sound
Of jubilation
I am the road to Zion
I arrived
In exaltation.

PONDER THE CROSS

A story well said
One of pain and dread
To the cross we are led
On our own accord
We are fed
The void of matter
We are invited
To shed.

Thy kingdom come on earth for some
Release the lame enlighten the dumb
The dread of the cross
Redeemed the loss
Be it done according to the word
Made flesh.

Arisen to light ascended in flight
My faith has restored my blinded sight
The cross I ponder
Perfection I wonder
What God has created
I am the I am
Well stated and perfectly mated.

STILL TODAY

Still today...tomorrow never came
The healing is now
Exclaims the leper and the lame
The day of old and the days of now
Are all the same
Harden not your heart
The spirit proclaimed
Encourage ourselves daily
While it is
Still today.

While still today
I am the come what may
The I am that I am
Is here to stay
Relinquish my soul
Separate me from decay
See me in the light
Of the purple ray.

Recognize me
I am absent
Rejoice with me
In my lament
Through your mercy
I am repent
Ascend my soul
From this earthly tent.

SUNSHINE ON MY FACE

Oh sunlight may I become you
May I become absent upon your face
May I pay no mind
To these days
But be the glory in your
Eternal haze.

The story of no time
The riddle with no rhyme
I am truth in the sublime
Grant me the faith to exist through time
Only as pure light
Will I shine.

Glory be to the Father Son and Holy Ghost
I am thy temple and thy host
May the sun shine on my face
Be it the symbol of your embrace
In mercy and humility
I plead my case.

A CELIBATE SPIRIT

Oh St. Anthony of celibate spirit
Call me from the desert...the desolate dirt
Call me from the poverty of riches
...From the depth of these trenches
....From this lowly place called the human race.

Sowing in poverty, enriched in grace
From the desert a celibate spirit I embrace
With the ear to hear
I see thy face
Depart from me dark night of the soul
A celibate spirit
Is in control.

A monk at will... a desire so real
An impoverished soul to thee revealed
An enlightened being no longer concealed
...Except to those
Who know me not.

ONLY HONOR

Only honor only praise
That I know not my days
But alas...only that my soul
Continue to honor and praise.

A calling is our nature
An answer is our cure
Desire and yearning is our lure
Only light so bright and so pure.

I have heard...I have seen
There is no other illumination in this dream
In the transformation into nothingness
There is sight unseen.

Only honor only praise
for the I am that I am
The only craze
In the rest of your days.

Joyce Marie Gilbert

A STREET CAR CALLED DESIRE

Oh desire! Thou art agony
A vehicle of intensity and ecstasy
A journey of joy and exubrancy
A destination called...
Within me.

A bright idea that never endS
That only a perfected state could send
Journey me away from the path of pretend
I am the pilgrim, I am thy vessel
I am the idea in the rehearsal.

Oh desire! Journey me through this transpire
Thou art agony thou art fire
I am the idea
In this street car named desire.

THE SABBATH WITHIN

Be the joyful hope
The still of peaceful waters
And be the rest in the Sabbath within
Repel anxiety...
That which we call sin.

Oh peace of soul I have arrived
Without you......
I would have not survived
Teach me the infinite
Teach me the divine
Teach me to be
Every moment
Thine.

The Sabbath within
I have birthed
Anxiety and restlessness
I have cursed
I am the joyful hope by which I cope
I am the Sabbath within
I rest in the still of peaceful waters
And in the infinite care
Of the eternal Father.

BLESS THE PEOPLE, OH LORD!

Bless the people oh Lord!
Our poverty is our afford
May our desire become our sword
And your blessing our reward.

The absence of thought
No one is taught....
But the search for you is what is sought
The I am....the redemption has been bought
The return from journey
Is our lot.

Rejoice oh people for we are blessed
The only God has laid us to rest
In the process we are the test...
But in the truth
We are the proof.

DEEP IS CALLING ON DEEP

In the deep you call on deep
Deeper yet is still to reap
Deep, deep down
Is much too steep
Is it me
You wish to see?

In this journey of the deep
Deep calls on deep to create and reap
The call of the wild is your child
Speak your OM so meek and mild
A gentle tug...to stay
Awhile.

Stay and rest in the deep beyond
No need to fear or run
In the journey....deep
You are the
The eternal Son.

Son of mercy
Son of man
Deep calls upon deep
To rest in the peace of eternal sleep.

THE SPIRIT OF POVERTY

Remove self from the corner shelf
It is I Lord who I cannot afford
My life is not of my accord....
But the Christ
Who is my reward.

In sickness and in health
My partner is not I
In this mirror there is no lie
For the Christ within
Is why I'm here to die.

Die to I the embellished self
The spirit of poverty is my sovereignty
I am the I am who set you free
...the I am that I am
That you now see.

SACRED SPACE

Oh Holy of Holies
May I be that sacred space
May I hold sacred the human race
I am the I am
Who appear in your face
....the Christ who pleaded your case.

Hold sacred my space
Hold steadfast my heart
I am the sum in all of your parts
I am thy
In thou art.

Rest in the womb of sacred space
Especially cradled for the chase
Express thyself beyond soft leather or fine lace
Thou art me in my image
Thou art free.

THE MOTION OF ENERGY

Where art thou going oh energy!
Are you matter or are you free
Do you matter or are you
Just me
If you're me it don't matter
...into dust I will scatter
...and my illusion
Will shatter.

The motion of energy
Is what I became
When I began to feed the lame
The truth I proclaim awakened from shame
Motion I am
Illusion I'm not
I am the arrival
Of what I sought.

WHAT SACRIFICE IS THIS

Oh what is this bliss?
A journey into the abyss
A soul never been kissed
A soul by-passed and missed.

What sacrifice is this
When carried through heavens
Undefiled like a child in the wild
A swift journey without pain or shame
Awakened and departed
From the land of the lame.

Sorry to have left
It felt like theft
But I must go
To where I know the peaceful waters flow.

Joyce Marie Gilbert

HERE I AM, THY WILL BE DONE

I've come to do your will
Shed these bones of human shield
Open the tabernacle once sealed
I am the I am who I call real.

Bless oh death, my eyes
For they have arrived
They have conceived myself as deprived
Reconcile me quickly before I rot
Have mercy on me
And forget me
Not.

I am here to do thy will
I am here on this window sill
To your loving kindness I appeal
To your oneness
I am here to become what you said
I am the manna from who I am fed.

BE THY SPACE

In my days may I be thy space
In thy space may I love the human race
The I am that I am.... the ram and the lamb
May I become your word in this land.

Only space can behold wisdom
Only wisdom can behold this system
I am the ponder oh God, I am the sought
May I become the word
That was sold and bought.

Be thy space in this Holy Land
Be thy beach without this sand
Be the God through the Son of Man!
Be the Word and so it is
I am the space in your human race.

TRANSCENDING MOVEMENT

How must that feel
...uniting the created spirit
With uncreated deity
A dark movement....a quiet one
One with no one around
A movement where nothing is found.

A bliss in a deep dark abyss
A joy in the soul never been kissed
A kiss never to be remembered or remissed
Thoughts of nothing in ponder
The fright of flight there is no wonder

Seek ye oh transcending servant
Find me here
Accepting thy repent.

WINTER IN PONDER

Still in ponder of winter wonder
Still lost in joyful splendor
A life given up in blissful render
I am presented as the worst offender.

Presented I am
And so it is
Created to be
Only free.

A seed in flight
No use for land
I am the I am
The generic brand.

CAST OUT FEAR

What city am I?
I am here to die
My soul does not lie
Oh my! I will die
...and I will fly.

Where fear is sought
Cast out its lot
I am not here to rot
I am here to live
Fear not.

What city am I?
Abraham awaits me there
I am the I am if I dare
I am the city for where
I must prepare
I am the city in whose eyes
I must stare.

TAMPERING WITH EVIDENCE

In your camp I tamper
In this bliss
I am the happy camper
I marvel at your presence in this being
I am the camper
Who tampers in the
Sight unseen.

The evidence is clear
I tamper without fear
I am this camp
In the journey less traveled
Into the mystery
To be unraveled.

Camping I love
Flying on the wings of a turtle dove
While tampering with evidence from above
Thomas Merton your journey was for certain
Tamper we must
Examining evidence in this dust
Happy campers we are
In this wonder lust.

Joyce Marie Gilbert

THE ENCOUNTER

Oh my goodness! In this place I thee wed
Oh ancient word speak what is being said
I am the temple that is being read
I am death that has been shed.

I am the encounter in the Holy Bread
The glimpse in the mirror led me here
Bless the transparency of this veil so very sheer
Bless the encounter... the Son of Man did appear

Rejoice oh people...in this temple we've been fed
It came to pass what's been said
The encounter is for both the living and the dead
It is especially for those who dread

Listen oh people!
The encounter is nigh...
....Lest you will die.

THE TOUCH OF THE HEART

The crowd is I
The touch was mine
Your garment I know
The threads I sew.

I am here stripped of fear
I left my tears and became a sear
With the touch of the heart
Thou did appear
My faith has saved me
This is clear.

Infinite ponder is where I reside
The touch of the heart is where I died
Arise little girl...
There I saw Jesus by my side
Awakened in truth
I became thy bride.
Yup! The touch of the heart
Is were heaven and earth collide

LIFE IN THE DAY OF THE ROCK

In the life of the rock there is no fame...
But upon this rock I build my church...
And upon this church I base my search
The sight unseen is the dream...
And the creation is all what it seems.

Life in the day of the rock
From what I found is what I sought
From what I created I only thought
Solid it is the truth be known
The sight unseen
Is what is shown.

The day of the rock is etched in stone
In faith the cover is blown
In God's image
I am cloned.

PONDER THE WONDER

Ponder the wonder
There is a down under...
But as for me
My heart grows fonder of the green grass
Up yonder.

Oh the dance of death
Is the best of me yet
The journey of old is mine
To unfold.

Prepare ye the way
I am life...from death I came
The dance of death is never to blame
Oh gladness you are greater than the sum whose
Kingdom has come.

MARY OH MOTHER

In thee I rest
With thee I attest
So many things kept in the heart
You brought forth that which I am a part.

A part I am the whole is me
The ponder is deep in the energy called Qi
Express me forth I am conception
Create me now
I know not deception.

I am your child in light
I am the memory in flight
I am the eyes who created sight
I am your heart in whole and in part.

PERCOLATION OF VIRTUE

Up through the heavens and down through my core
The sound of grace is the knock at my door
7 up 7 down
Listen to the percolating sound in its core
The sound in my feet is gushing to the street
The percolation of virtue is my soul complete.

Oh soul Divine, thou art so kind
To percolate in this body of mine
7 up 7 down
I am the chakras in my mind
I am the vessel where you reside
I am the spirit who never died.

DEEP SEEDS

Toil down deep
Where golden seeds reap
Where riches are yours to keep...
And the drops of heavenly waters seep.

Toil the deep
Study the sun worship the moon
You will be home soon.

Toil the soil
Anoint thyself with sacred oil
Ponder the deep
Where golden seeds reap...
And riches are yours to keep.

Come one come all
Behold your home
Where all your heavenly seeds are sown.
Ponder the deep
Where golden seeds reap
And riches from heaven
Are yours to keep.

OH LOSS

Thy inventory I take
To find I'm drowning in this lake
I create pinnacles to hold on to fate
I am sensitive to every move you make.

Oh loss we must depart
I can no longer hold you dear to my heart
Detach we must
No longer can we lust
One must fly
The other must return to dust.

Thanks for the dine...
But you are no longer mine
Depart from me
You are now freed
Free to attach yourself to whoever you may be
As for me, I am the bride
Of the Divine.

BEFORE THEE I STAND

Before thee I am
Before thee I stand...
At the ark of the promised land
My appearance is my request
Accept thy servant at this event.

I am the appearance in the womb of the Christ
I am the I am who was bought for a price
I am the I am who honors your rule
I may not be cool...
But I ain't no fool
I am your student in your
Wisdom school.

THE WOMAN WHO SPEAKS

I speak to you oh God!
I am not afraid of your staff and rod
I am not shy to speak about the dogs under the table
I am not one to consider the gospel a fairy tale
My faith is my voice
In my body I rejoice
In your image I am
Poised.

I am the woman who speaks
I am the I am who I seek
I am the woman in the mirror
Whose sight is not seen...
But whose slate is wiped clean.

How grateful am I!
...that I'm called to die in the absence of the lie
Grateful I am
Humbled to face grace alone
I am the women who speaks
From home.

APART FROM ME

Apart from me is your communion
Depart from me my only son...
For I am not needed in this reunion
Only You are needed
Please be seated in my life
Which I have deeded.

Quiet I know
Peaceful I am
I am dust awaiting in lust...
For the moment in time
To become sublime
Oh Adam I know
In the garden I sow
The seed I am whose blood is the lamb.

Dust is my return
I am not needed where you're concerned
Apart from me
Is what I've learned
The soil is I ...
And I am you
Alas! I have risen
From the many to the very few.

THE GARDEN OF DELIGHT

Oh suffering in the night
You are the backbone of this flight
You remain constant delivering your light
Without you
I would never be right.

You are my one and only
There is but one sorrow...
And that is to have lost
The garden of delight.

Without you
I would never know there is but one hope and one desire
To recover that which was lost once prior

Oh garden of delight
Return to me this sight
I am the I am
Who finished this flight
In the dark of night.

I TRULY KNOW

Oh conqueror I truly live
By the food you give
In this moment I truly know
You've conquered deception for me below.

The battle is won for me
I no longer have to fight deception to be free
Silence is won
The prince of peace has come
No longer must I encounter
The defeat of the dumb.

Lay slain is thy master
If only I could have known much faster
It is what it is
I rejoice and truly know
I only reaped
What I sewed.

THE PONDER OF THE DAY

The altar of your heart
Is where I start
Where my gaze is upon thou art
I am your sum in whole and in part.

The ponder of the day
Is in the word that you say
It is in the wisdom for which I pray
It is in the joy that you are here to stay

Forget me not as I wait in ponder...
For in your truth there is no wonder
In defeat of deceit I can be no prouder
In the I am
I could be no fonder.

OH HAPPY DAY

Ashes to ashes dust to dust
I am no longer on the cusp
Dried bones are enlightened
Exultation heightened ...
The hidden fruit has ripened.

Oh happy day! You are my sunshine
At this table I will dine
In my season this hidden fruit is beyond reason.

Beyond joy I employ
Nothing I could imagine
Could satisfy this passion.

Oh happy day! Color me gone
I am sacrificed for all to see
...but as for me
I have gone to be with thee.

BLESS THE MOMENT

Strip away what nature loves
Resist the temptation of turtle doves
See the gulls grappling for fish heads on the shore
The lion roars but he knows not what for
Nature is itself... and cannot be more.

Remove thyself from this limit
In this void thou must commit
In this haunted place thou must sit...
...Until which time
Your soul is snatched from the pit.

Bless this moment thou has sent
It is the encounter of what is said and all that is meant
Fortunate soul, fear nothing
The search for the Divine has found its match
Bless this moment of nature's detach
'Tis the moment you've been snatched.

MORE OF THE SAME

Here remains sacks of grief like stones
Ears are badgered with lies and moans
Eyes that only see with rods and cones
Hearts that must be broken
And beg to be shown.

Today I fast in deep repent
Today I bask in great lament...
For I am lowly as I present
...but your favor is upon me on this day of lent.

Mea culpa mea culpa
Who I am is not what I sought
I empty myself in the trough
Dressed in this human sack of cloth

More of the same
I am to blame...
But in your mercy
I am the person
For who you came.

REPAIRER OF THE BREACH

I am called the repairer of the breach
In your truth through Isaiah I beseech
From my midst I have removed oppression and malice
speech
Light has risen from darkness upon my reach.

Gloom has become like mid-day....
Total illumination of your Son's rays
My strength is renewed
My debt has been paid
The foundations from ages past I have raised up
Ancient ruins are rebuilt for my sake
Restorer of ruined homesteads I have become.

The ride on the heights of the earth is my new birth
Incline your ear oh Lord
For I am afflicted and poor
In your mercy I beseech
I'm in search for the Repairer of the breach.

THE BATTLE OF THE ANGELS

'Tis the season in the desert
Darkness in the soul sees no light
'Tis the season of temptation where evil is its plight
Be mindful
The battle of angels is the sight
Be mindful
The battlefield be not judged
Nor the bloodshed begrudged.

Steadfast be still and know
The battle of angels is not for show
Their authority is over the low
They render salvation here below.

Minister....
As mindfulness becomes me
Guide me into stillness while the battle rages
Protect me as I fly with you through the ages
I am the I am
The spoken word of these pages.

DEPARTURE OF JUDGEMENT

A moment in repent...I present this lent
Depart from me oh judgment
I am the I am who was sent
Forever and always it is the law of love for why I lament
...but in this mindfulness
I live in content.

Depart from me oh judgment
For you are not He
Present oh God the law of love in lieu of me
Oh humbled heart
Bless my repent for this I lament
Forever and always I will live
This content.

Oh the joy of contentment
Thou art my reign
Solely in you does my life pertain
Forgiven I am, grateful is she
To be given the law of love in this century.

INTEGRES GRACE

Integres grace
I am your voice
May I become thy choice
From where I rejoice.

Infinite light
A motion in flight
I am your eyes that breathes so kind
I am the blind who leads your mind
I am thy grace who takes your place.

Quiet the hush
The more quite it is
Quite the rush
The more stillness can be
I am that grace that unites me to thee.

OH FAULT!

Without thee I wouldn't be me
Nor a shadow would I see
Only the self, fighting to be free
Oh fault! Thou hast revealed your decree.

You have imparted yourself to sacrifice
Quite honorably you've given thyself for the price
You've acknowledged your worth and all of its strife
Thank you oh fault!
From your sacrifice my life is derived.

Separation is tough, the loss is great
But you understand
Oh fault! It must be fate.
Gladden your heart as I enter the gate
Rejoice, for in your gift
I am the bride and God is my mate.

PRAYER WITHOUT A PRAYER

Look upon me without a prayer
As sandstone speaks not of its layers
As a dust storm speaks not of its dust
...as a lowly pilgrim whose reliance on God is a must.

A prayer without a prayer
Is my soul clothed in nakedness...
how dare her...become a constant plea....
a constant request to be
No not me.

The constant knock becomes the door
The prayer without a prayer is no more
Reliance on God is constant...
Like a request to be...
No not me.

THE QUIET MIND

Woe! Is me, for I am not
The quiet mind in which I sought
I am not the quiet mind my birth has brought
Nor the one I once thought.

Have mercy on my egocentrism...
For I did not know I was imprisoned
My self was upon me...
For in the forest there grows no tree.

In the center of self I could not see
There is no other seen by me
Until the quiet mind did appear
I never knew the other in the mirror
Could be so dear.

EXTEND TO THOSE

My desire is my heart on fire
Love not the lie, but the liar
Love not the action, but the intent prior
Guile belongs not in the Towne Crier.

Love belongs to the enemy that is mine
Love belongs to the enemy with whom I dine
I must extend to those for whom I am not inclined
Perfect me not in what I've sought...
But in the perfect love your Son has brought.

Extend to those to whom You chose
Your Father's love and why You rose
Perfect this love in me...so that in your image I may be
The one who extends to those
Who can not see.

THE SHINING CLOUD

The voice from the shining cloud speaks
An ancient call to the humble and meek
My face in the shining cloud is who I seek
The perfected image is the hope that I keep.

Justice and mercy is the controversy
Or did the son of many come from New Jersey
The voice from the shining cloud speak
Speak the Word incarnate to the Sephardic.

Speak! For the breath of life hears
Arise...for the Son of Man appears
Provide my daily bread in the arrears
I remember now...the ancient call...the fall...and the
apostle Paul

Oh voice in the shining cloud speak!
I am the I am who you seek
I am the humble, I am the meek.

THE NAKED EYE

Oh see thyself, oh naked eye
Wretched and pathetic in your evil lie
Defecate on to yourself
You will never die
The liar is your witness
Deception is your kiss.

I am the I am who judges you not
But only observes your destruction and rot
I am the spectator whose nakedness is your core
...Awaiting in observance for your repentance
once more.

Oh see thyself, oh naked eye
Behind the fig leaf, don't be shy
Seek your truth abandon your lie
I am the I am who hears your cry
Abandon the lie... truth does not die.

STILL ME

Still me...
For I am present
My vibration I cannot prevent
The joy of God and the agony of lent is my lament
Hold me in this state...
In the stillness... I create.

I am one with the ONE
I am the one called Son
Still me...
For I am present
Hear me for I am listening
Bless me for I have sinned.

Consider me passioned for my desire to be rationed
Clothe me in courage; although not highly fashioned
Fill me with joy in the still of the night
Accept me now by the sweat of my brow.

I WALK WITH THEE

It is our day today
I walk the Dolorosa with thee
Bring forth this reality
May it be known to me.

Love me for I am present
Shine your light for I am bright
Bring light to Brookdale for they are your people
In all homes extend a steeple.

Bring passion to my soul
Provide life...for it is told
Provide love...for it is cold
Bring forth thy peace
In this union of Holy Communion
May we all find rest in your case.

DO NOT TOUCH ME

Do not touch me...
For I am He
Do not hold on to me...
For I am gone.
Your faith is where I'm from
I've returned to kingdom come.

The faithful in my day saw where I was laid
They were taught much about not being afraid
They were taught much about touch and such
...without flesh...without caress.

For sacrifice is itself its debt
It must be paid as it was laid
It must be read as it was said
Rest in peace for He is dead.

Do not touch me...for I am gone
Do not grieve for I am free
In mercy and in grace
I have prepared you a place that my garment has replaced.

Joyce Marie Gilbert

THE BREATH IN THE STORM

Oh breath! Thou art the eye in my storm
Be mindful...
For I am not forlorn
I am thee...
Calm, peaceful, and reborn.
I am newly created morn' after morn'.

Enjoy with me your silent rhythm
Breathe with me for I am thee
For in the midst of this storm we are free
Breathe with me... breathe with me
I am He.

In communion I dwell
In this storm I propel
Thou art the eye of my cry
And the cradle of my sigh
Breathe with me...breathe with me
I am He.

OF THIS I KNOW

Be this...
For I may know
This quiet moment, please bestow
For it is You... this I know
Be here with me
Below.

Breathe easy...
See my soul, for it has reached great heights.

A place of rest
A place to be
I am the I am in me
I am the place that I see
I can attest to the land called free.

Ahh, my Lord
This test I did not pass on my accord
This splendor I could not afford...but
You carried me to this place
Of reward.

DO NOT BE ANGUISHED

Peace at hand
No agitation in this land
A profound peace supersedes the torment in the flesh
Be not frightened or suppressed.

Express yourself in love for God
Take up your cross, your staff and rod
Leave Babylon
The mountain is your sod...
Your peace is your God.

Agitation be gone
My mountain is my lawn
I've trekked and trekked
But still not gone
I await this fate...
This peace....this calm.

CALM THY MIND

Quiet oh soul
The mind is but a mole
A chip off the ole block...
A speck of sand upon a rock.

Calm thy mind
To its madness be ever so kind
Respect its creation...
But it need not cast its manifestation .

Quiet oh soul
For thou art finished
No need to fret
Nothing to regret
...Only love paid this debt.

Joyce Marie Gilbert

ALLOW THYSELF TO BE TIRED

Be tired
Allow the ego to be fired
Allow thyself to retire
Lay dead in the street
Allow all to trample
As you feel them at your feet
Greet them with defeat.

Feel exhausted and withered
Feel dehydrated and incapacitated
For this moment, your flesh has been slated
For this moment, time has been dated.

Allow thyself to feel tired
Fire your ego...for she was your only amigo
But in this moment, lift thy eyes...
For your soul has been glorified
And admired.

PASS

Oh breeze pass!
No matter how slow or fast
In the present or in the past
Full sail or half mast
Oh breeze... pass!

No need to pass go
No need to fret... to and fro
Just pass... breeze.... pass!

No need to speak or know
No need for fancy or show
Pass... breeze... pass... far beyond the ugly black crow
This is your last hurrah here below
Pass.... breeze... pass!

ST. CATHERINE

Be my mind for me
I hear you speak so triumphantly
I want to know thy grace
That is written on my face
I want to write about this embrace.

I know the dark side of dark...
But sometimes dark is dark and there is no other walk
In this park.

Whether in darkness or in light
You are fed your daily bread
Your Holy will is protected...
Even tho not detected.
Your sacrifice has been accepted.

Thank you St. Catherine
For breathing words into a soul
whose sight has been so affected
By the darkness in flight.

BLESS THE CHILDREN

Oh blessings and growth,
Stagnation or motion, it can't be both
Retardation or enlightenment
Bless the children that God sent
For his glory is why these lives are meant.

Bless these children
For they are pure
They await your eternal cure
Awaken them through light
Dispel confusion and their fright.

Alas! the cure... the commitment sure
To the eternal end we will endure
Bless these children for they are ONE
Free us from this desert...
For our kingdom has come.

OH FATHER!

Appear oh Father when nothing is near
Consider my efforts to strip this fear
Transform this heart
For the veil is sheer
Consider my will for it is truth...
But consider me absent and not here.

Appear oh Father when nothing is near
Consider my strife of death in this mirror
Consider me gone
I've been the I am all along
Rejoice in me and grant me this song
I am the I am
Neither right nor wrong.

Appear oh Father when nothing is near
Accept my will with a bottomless cheer
Consider me gone
For it is truth
I am here
But I am gone
Please accept me in my birthday suit.

A PERSONAL TRAIT

I am the trait of my mate
Dispel the falsehood of my fate
Take from me my will...
For I am not real
Loyalty to God is a personal trait
For this I appeal.

A personal trait in heart and mind
A perfected mate to house the Divine
With this trait I thee wed
With your grace I am fed.

Rejoice in me, for I am Yours
Root in me the cure of all cures
Remain in me that I may endure
Accept my trials and tribulations
For I am pure.

THE INTERFACE

Oh may this interface never fade
May this matrix be permanently laced
If gaps and holes...pay no mind
It's the interface that is a joy to find.

In my mind of the human kind
Imprint the matrix of this spiritual find
Witness with me the spaces as they shrink...
Help me to realize I'm on the brink.

Remember this joy with me
Remember the matrix of this spiritual find
Remember this on the deathbed of human kind
But today...the day of my joy
May I employ this vision whose matrix is unseen
May I share with them this vision of the Holy dream.

A BLESSED BLOW

Strike my pride...
Until my ego is fried
Oh hand of God strike me with your rod
Destroy every inkling of this fraud
Chastise me again
I welcome the apprehend.

Destroy esteem
I am the I am, not who I seem
Recognize in me your image... the Supreme
Awaken me with this blessed blow... from this dream
Moment by moment
Day by day
Poem by poem
I thee wed, oh blessed blow
Accept this seed that I sow
Here below.

PASS ON

Pass on for it is good
All isn't what it looks...
But all is as it should
Pass on, pass on oh mighty one
All the work is said and done.

All light is passing in the dark
The dark night of the soul has come
No worries, no fret
All saints can attest
There is no loss
There is no debt
The lights are dim the stage is set.

A time to mourn, a time to pass
Pass on, pass on oh mighty one
Thy soul is great, you have met your mate
This is your time you must create.

THE GRACE OF NAKEDNESS

Bless my nakedness
...for it is Holy Grace
In my reflection may I see not my face
I wish not to remember the time or place
Strip me naked
...for faith is sacred.

The vision of quest is my Sunday best
The grace of nakedness in thee I rest
I sit in quiet...watching, waiting...stripping
May I watch every last drop of blood
Dripping, dripping...dripping.

Oh grace of nakedness
Fill this empty vessel
May I never again wrestle
Gaze my eye on the dazzle
Never to see my face
Or remember the time or the place.

DANCE OH MORNING!

Leap for joy this is not a toy
This reality I employ
The intercession of Mary I enjoy.

Intercede oh Mother
Your grace was never lost
No judgment or lament
Through you, God was sent.

Dance oh morning!
To the Mother of God I cling
It is her praises that I dance and sing
Dance oh morning!
Dance to the sound of the bells that ring
Protect this journey back
To the Son of God Supreme.

ASCEND

Remove the gaze from this purple haze
Extract me from this maze
Release time from my days.

Ascend me forth
Blazing in this painful torch
I know no other
...only Father and Mother
Who lifts my nature from this creature.

Ascend I am
Arisen I know
Lost from self is the seed I sow
Conquer this death from me below
This gift for man
I wish bestowed.

ASK FOR ME

Through the Son
I am chosen
Ask for me... that joy may be fulfilled.

Fulfill the joy
That only the Godhead can employ
Ask for me... so that I may enjoy
This I ask
That the Son of Man
Remove my mask.

Ask for me
And it will be done for me to see
A desire like no other to know my Father
A dream opposite of what it seems
A reality to be lived and all what it means.
A joy fulfilled in the Supreme.

OIL OF GLADNESS

Anoint this drop of sadness
With the oil of gladness
Place this drop on the eve of madness
Place the sign of the cross
In this place of loss.

Oh my Jesus forgive us our sins
Save us from the fires of hell
Lead all souls into heaven
...especially those in most need of thy mercy.

The oneness is our gladness
The son of destruction is our sadness
Create discernment... dissolve madness
Recognize the cross in this well of loss.

...While the tomb is empty
The cross remains
Rejoice oh children, the oil of gladness has removed all
sadness.
A drop has been placed on the eve
Of this madness.

PRAY OH GOD!

Pray oh God for my family and these people
Love them oh God
That they may reside in your steeple
The son of destruction be gone!
Thou art powerless amongst
The strong.

Lift the fog oh God
On this eve of destruction
Present thyself in the sacrament of Extreme Unction
Do not let the dawn fall upon this soul
I trust that your loving mercy is in control.

It is my intention to pray oh God
For my family and these people
That they reside in your steeple.
Heal oh God all that is false
And kindly remove your thumb from this pulse.

GLORY IN THE WORLD

Glory is the air we breathe
Not only in the heavens but on the earth...
Glory is and will be
The chance we take... the love we make
There is but one reality, the rest is fake.

Glory me now, for I am real
For this joy... I appeal
Forgive this creature in my nature
I am the I am
I am Glory in this story.

In the glory of the World
There is truth in the sword
Place me forth in the front lines
if it is your will to search their minds

Peace I know
In glory I sing
The glory in the world
Is what I bring.

IN THE STILLNESS

Quiet the day
For this I pray
Remove this world
From where I speak and say.

Remove this world
I need not be jeweled or pearled
In the stillness I am clothed
Be still and know
That I am God
In this stillness know
There is no façade.

In the stillness
There is only realness
Nothing to see, nothing to feel
Know that I am God
In nothingness accept your joyfulness.

SELF REVENGE

Self revenge
A resolve for all amends
A truce for the battle against God
A peace that acknowledges it's fraud.

Bless this self revenge
It is me you may apprehend
It is I whose self, I deny
It is I who hears the cry.

Feed my lambs, oh Peter
The only way to love God is to feed them
Revenge thyself for the extent of thy wealth
I will bear onto you
Upon that which you do.

THIS SUFFERING

...does not end
It's called your friend
Joy and suffering is the blend
There is no pretend.

Bless this suffering
For it is good.
Allow me understanding as I should
May the strength flow through me
Pass on oh Mother
To your heavenly Father
Your merciful love I plea.

Oh Paraclete be with those who suffer
Shine forth your grace
In this joy I plea this case
This suffering is my only praise
Accept from me my lowly hands and heavenly gaze.

OH PARACLETE

My dread you know
From where your spirit flows
Moment by moment
I live this parchment in lament.

Bring to your Father this sacrifice
May it be for me a plea of suffice
May it be for me the love of the Christ
Upon this altar, accept my falter
On this dread I could not be fonder.

Smile the smile of completion
May I rest in the peace of this feast
May your wonder never cease
May my faith grow in strength
And may this steep incline
Only increase.

PRAY OH GOD

Your presence I ask
My prayer oh God is behind this mask
Sit with the dying... no one else can
Touch this death with the blood of the lamb
Transform this death into the Son of Man.

Pray oh God!
Receive the dying
We are crying
We are your gift of dread
We are the glory that is yours
In your time we await your anointing
of Holy cures.

The dread is yours
In your Spirit it is fed
On this day may she be wed
Into your hands may she become your Holy Bread.

OMMISSIONS AND COMMISSIONS

What I've done and failed to do
Bless what I know to be true
Lead me Jesus into the suffering you went through
Remove this fear
So that your Father may appear.

My omissions and commissions I know them
I am the crowd
I am they who condemn
I am those bones who cry out
From the hallows of Sheckem
Hear me oh Father
Suffer with my mother, brother and sister
And me.

Commission me now remove this frown
For in this joy I contemplate this Holy crown
In stillness
I listen...listen....for this sound.

Joyce Marie Gilbert

THIS ECLIPSE

The shadow of death
The agony of breath
This eclipse slowly arrives
...taking life
And leaving the knife.

Slowly, slowly suffering becomes

The soul has no name
It matters not if you're sane or lame
The fight is deadly
The death is costly

...but this Eclipse
Will never be undermined
...for in this dungeon
All are kind.

SALUTE TO DARKNESS

Observe with stillness
Peel an eye for its realness
Do not make a sound...or thrash about
There is no other route.

Enter its mouth
Seek its clutches and its couch
Prepare yourself for this route
Every day the darkness will shed light
Moment by moment observe its flight.

To the darkness I salute
To its end I resolute
I stand alone and smile at its face
I bring peace and find rest
In describing it to the human race.

THE JOY IN YOUR NAME

In your name I am
In bondage I am the lamb
But... the joy in your name
Has released me from being lame
I walk from where I came
...out of a family....and I have no shame.

Oh happy day! I am not dead
I arise with joy and I sleep in dread
Father in your name I am the joy
Who heard this call
I am the joy who suffered this fall.

Tell me more while I soar
Show me the depth at its core
Suffering and death is knocking at my door

Joy answers.

ON THIS DAY

Oh my Jesus forgive us our sins
Save us from the fires of hell
And lead all souls into heaven
...especially those in most need of thy mercy.

Accept this family as an act of sacrifice
The only human gift I have to offer...
Is the one where I truly suffer.

Unite us with your Holy Spirit
Accept our family together...in merit
Look not upon our faults, but upon
The faith of those who share it.

SECRET RESURRECTIONS

This moment of sorrow
Brings forth the Christ of tomorrow
In sin we are the tombs where the Christ
Lies dead
...but in sorrow we are the Christ that removes death
from our bone marrow.

In sorrow life is renewed
The first sign of repentance
The fog is lifted from a place called dense.
Awareness is given...a paradise for the livn'
And all is forgiven.

Secret resurrections I know them
There are many
Each dancing to and fro
Oh the joy and the witness
Watching the seeds grow.
Arise, arise oh secret resurrections
Be glad and rejoice
Welcome yourself
To the God of perfection.

THE LOVE OF EMPTYNESS

No fulfillment will suffice
A total misunderstanding of the sacrifice
Misperception will be my demise
But as for me
There will be no compromise.

The love of emptiness
Is where I go
The depth of sorrow
Is what I know.

I know not what they see
But the love of emptiness is for me
This dissension will continue
The disconnect is read right off the menu
The persecution is in silence
From a family on the fence.

On the fence is a perch
On the perch is no search
Without experience there is no church
Color me gone
...for nothing has been left undone.

Remember me not
For the love of emptiness is my lot
It is the grave in which I sought
It is the glory that I was taught
...but all in all
It is You that I love a lot.

RAISE A GLAD CRY

For Zion is our mother now
Bless this offer for it is Yours
We are your children
We dance and sing
We are home.

On this Holy mountain
This gate is preferred by the Lord
To all of Jacob's dwellings
Raise this glad cry
Hear this mountain tremble with joy.

It is your children who knock
We're here with our mother
We ask if you would unlock this gate
Oh Zion.... accept this transformation.

We raise our glad cry
In You our heart sighs!

LISTEN OH GOD

Hear thyself for thou art near
You fill me with tithing and good cheer
You ask that I look in the mirror
You speak about no fear.

I hear
...but what about suffering
Will you explain that good cheer?
No matter
I am your people, I wait in this steeple
Listen oh God! Jerusalem speaks
We're still moaning about the 7 weeks.

Listen oh God your people suffer
Listen for how or why
You want to make it rougher

I listen...I wait
I praise with respect and honor
And lament.

Until the moment you apprehend
I bask in your Son called friend
Through my nervous system you won't pretend
I'll know the answers to my questions
You wish to send.

...like tonight...the day of her death
You are in my nervous system
Holding all portals open
Pouring Holy Chrisom.

An occasion such as this
I celebrate with everyone in the abyss
Listen oh God....
I am listening....

CORPUS CHRISTY

This sacrifice I honor
Of this redemption
I could not be fonder
I am lowly
But I am yours
Into this cup my spirit assures.

The spirit of your creation
Is me in this damnation
Accept from my hands
My mother from this land
I am lowly
I am sand
...but raise us up with this cup.

Corpus Christy
Cover us with the blood of the lamb
Proclaim us the I am
In communion with sacrifice
In this union we ask not to be chastized
Take our gift of spirit
'tis our only gift of merit.

LOST IN THE ONE WHO PROVOKES MY AWE

Look upon my awe with gaze
As I remain steadfast through all my days
Accept this wonder I ponder
Never to return
To my concern.

The dead will bury the dead
The dread will not be said
..but I in wonder...I do ponder
In awe
Of what I saw.

Stillness at the gate
I've been gifted my fate
Suffering...inevitable
Horror...unimaginable
...but I've been gifted...
Lost in the ONE who provokes my awe.

A DAY OF BURIAL

Receive this day
At your feet I pray
Be this as it may
Bring forth love
As she lay.

Peace brother to the whole world
May the suffering heal thy sword
Arise oh lame and the bored
May we be blessed by this accord.

Receive oh Lord
Our sacrifice for it is good
Accept our mother from our land
Oh Jerusalem we are your children
....and you are now our mom and dad.

A GOOD FRIDAY

Let the dead bury their dead
Leave behind death and all its dread
Arise oh Word and all it says
In power and glory
No tear is shed.

Today is the day the Lord has made
Today is the day
I am not afraid.
Today is Good Friday the day you paid
I no longer am enslaved
...but glorified through the price of sacrifice.

Take from me this cup
Gladly to give up
Humbly I praise thee
I am your daughter
I am not me
...but thee.

MY MOTHER

Oh mother Mary
This is not contrary
...but explanatory
This is not the tooth fairy
...but visionary.

A strange phenomenon,
To contemplate your Son
...but you kept ALL in your heart
...Including me
Which I am a part.

You are my mother now
Place this sweat upon my brow
Place this crown of jewels upon my frown
Hold my smile forever in your womb
I am your child
I have been reconciled.

RETURN OH MOTHER

Save the day for this one
Today is the day the Lord has made
We are with you, mother
In this motorcade
We are faithful
We are courageous
....And not afraid.

Return oh mother to your final resting place
Shine forth the image of God's face
For this glory we elude our human race
Bestow your patience on us
For this snail's pace.

Return oh mother
We wait
Illuminate for us our path of fate
In your sacrifice we appreciate
Return to dust
If you must
...but in this fuss
It is our God we honor
With this cup.

THE DAY AFTER

The day after...
Bring forth laughter
No need for shatter;
Although nothing could be sadder

Steadfast in salvation
The day after...
Is nothing more than
Another day after.

The resurrection I wish to master
Surround me in joy
Oh Rita and Eloy
Protect me oh parents
From all laments.

A complete union is our communion
Arise oh children from this dread
This day after
May you eat this bread
May you love our God
And believe what
Is said.

About The Author

Joyce maintains a daily meditative writing practice which consists of a written prayer, a blessing, and a poem. Her collection to date consists of over 700 pages of such writings. This simple practice is done in contemplation in the absence of cognitive thought; and is one of many techniques that promote physical, mental and spiritual wellness.

Her writings have been well cultivated by Fr. Fran Dorff, a Mystic, Philosopher, and published author in residence at the Norbertine Abbey, Albuquerque, New Mexico; and by Sister Paula Gallagher, also a published author, and Liturgist for the Archdiocese of Santa Fe. As a student, Joyce has had the great privilege of studying their published works and attending their many writing workshops, seminars, and mentorship programs through the years.

Joyce holds a Certification in Spiritual Direction from the Benedictine Monastery of Guadalupe in Pecos, New Mexico, and maintains a private practice assisting others in their journey to integrate body, mind and spirit through meditative writing and other techniques.

Along with a Bachelor's Degree in Health, a Master's Degree in Public Health, and a Doctoral Certificate from the Institute of Meta Psychology, Joyce holds a Diploma in Natural Therapeutics, and has been in private practice for the last 32 years as a licensed Massage Therapist specializing in trauma based injury.

www.ingramcontent.com/pod-product-compliance
Lightning Source LLC
Chambersburg PA
CBHW072007060426
42446CB00042B/2126